EASY PIANO

Monty Python's SPAMALOT™

CONTENTS

ISBN 978-1-4234-1008-9

HAL•LEONARD®
CORPORATION
7777 W. BLUEMOUND RD. P.O. BOX 13819 MILWAUKEE, WI 53213

Visit Hal Leonard Online at
www.halleonard.com

KING ARTHUR'S SONG

Lyrics by ERIC IDLE
Music by JOHN DU PREZ and ERIC IDLE

Pompously brisk

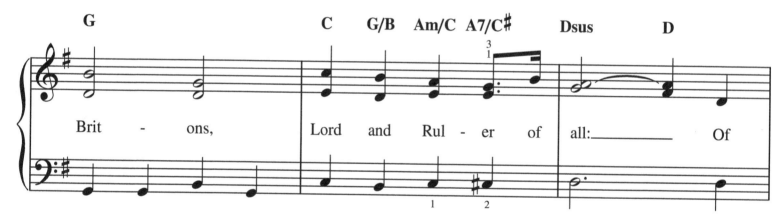

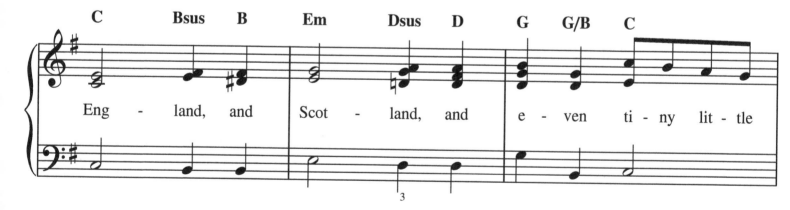

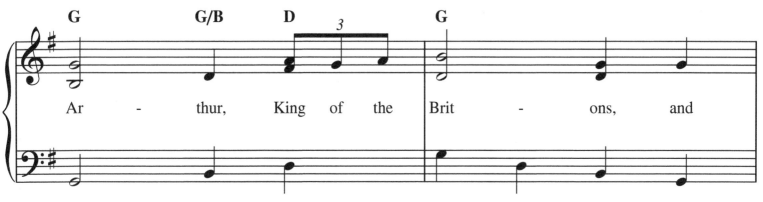

Ar - thur, King of the Brit - ons, and

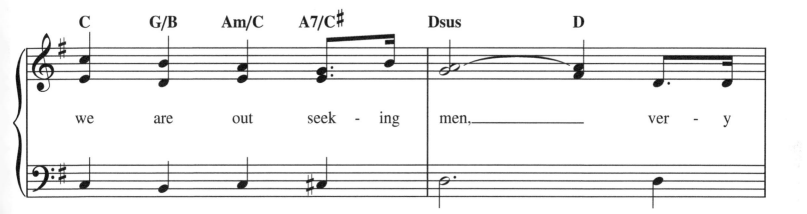

we are out seek - ing men,_____ ver - y

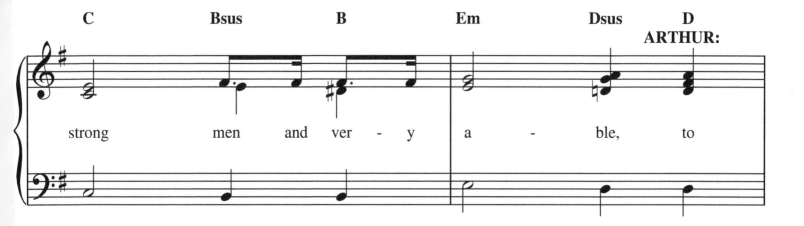

strong men and ver - y a - ble, to

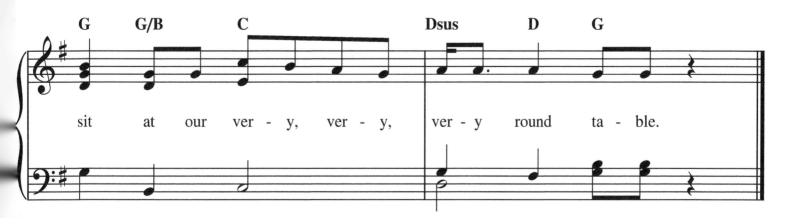

sit at our ver - y, ver - y, ver - y round ta - ble.

FINLAND/FISCH SCHLAPPING DANCE

FINLAND
Words and Music by
MICHAEL PALIN

FISCH SCHLAPPING DANCE
Words by ERIC IDLE
Music by JOHN DU PREZ and ERIC IDLE

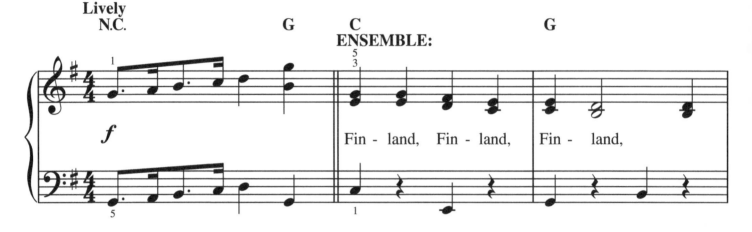

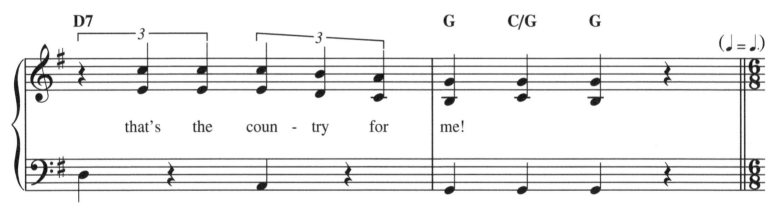

that's the coun-try for me!

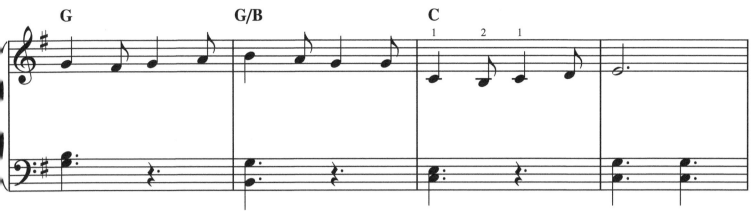

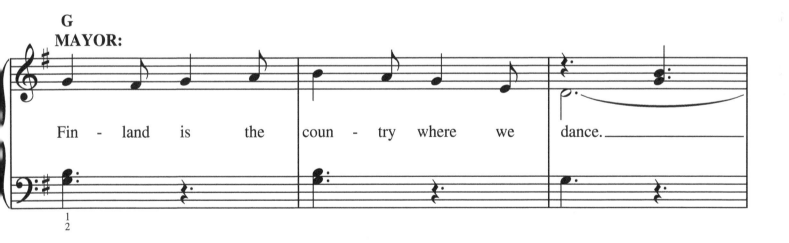

Fin - land is the coun - try where we dance. ____

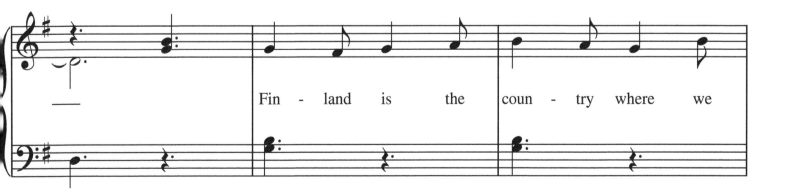

____ Fin - land is the coun - try where we

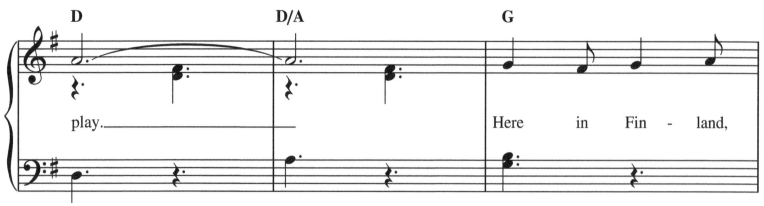

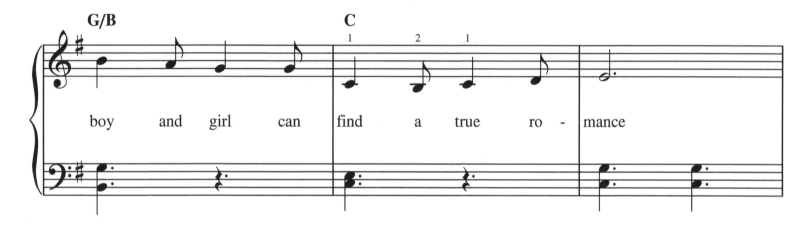

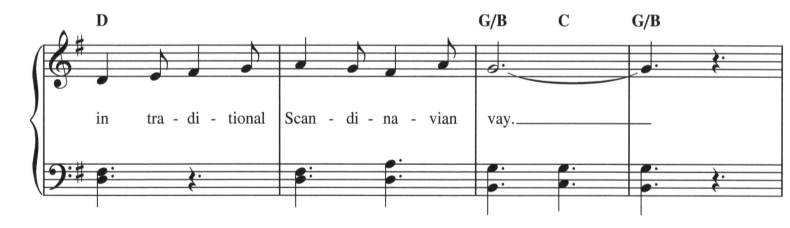

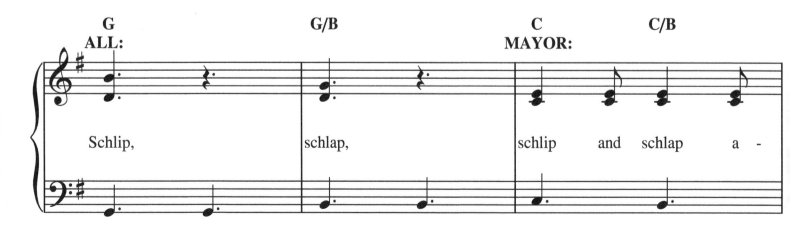

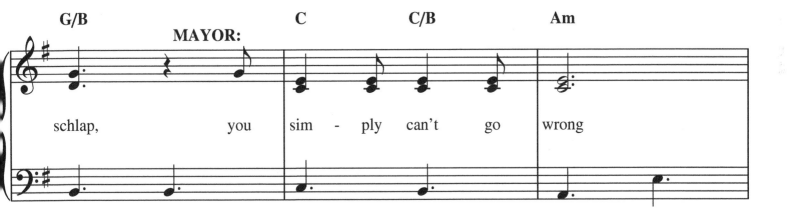

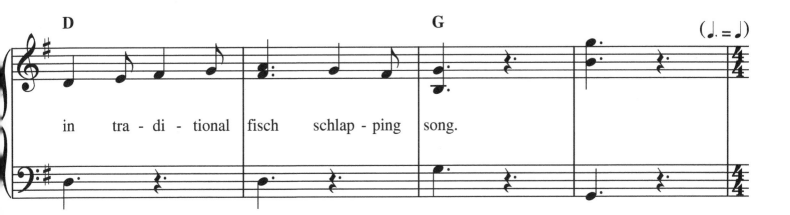

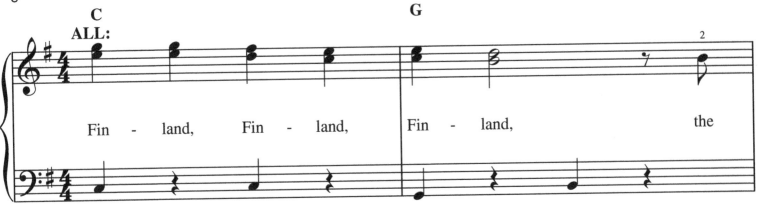

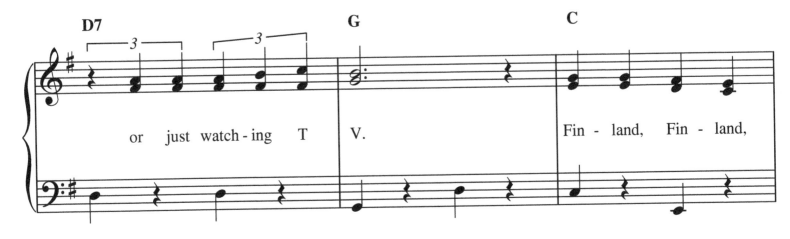

HE IS NOT DEAD YET

Lyrics by ERIC IDLE
Music by JOHN DU PREZ and ERIC IDLE

Moderate Polka

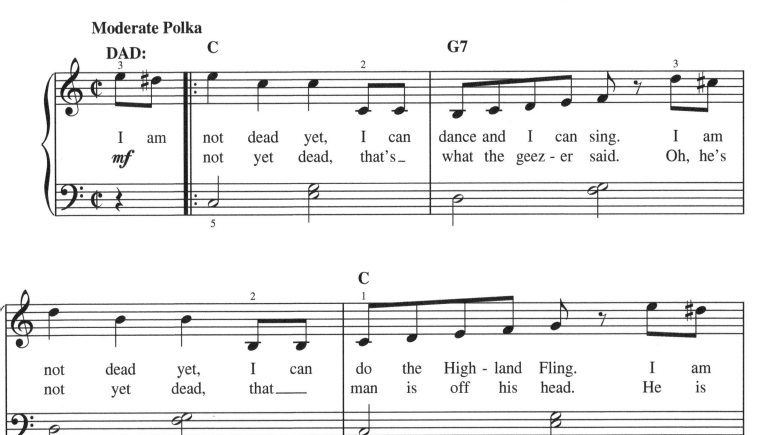

2.

C   F   C/E   N.C.   C

not yet dead.   *Lancelot whacks Dad on the head.*   Well, now he's dead. You

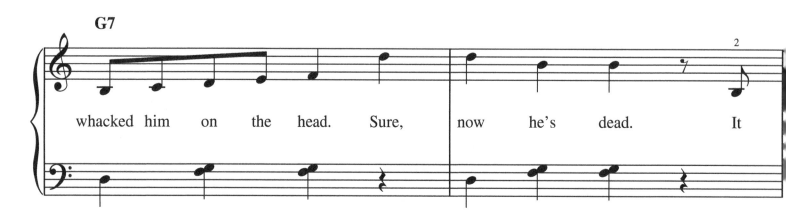

G7

whacked him on the head. Sure, now he's dead. It

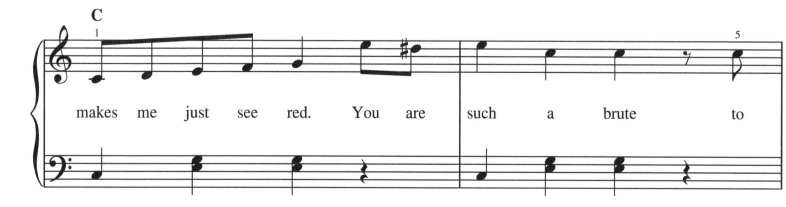

C

makes me just see red. You are such a brute to

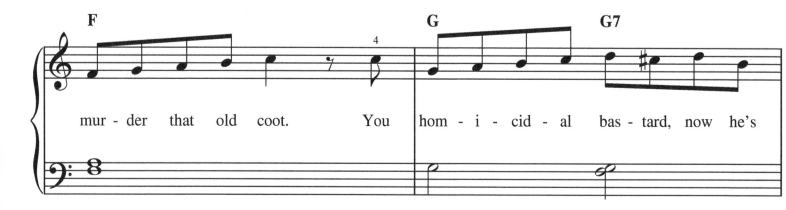

F   **G**   **G7**

mur - der that old coot. You hom - i - cid - al bas - tard, now he's

real - ly dead. Who is the knave who put him in his grave and who

LANCELOT:

needs to man - age his an - ger? My

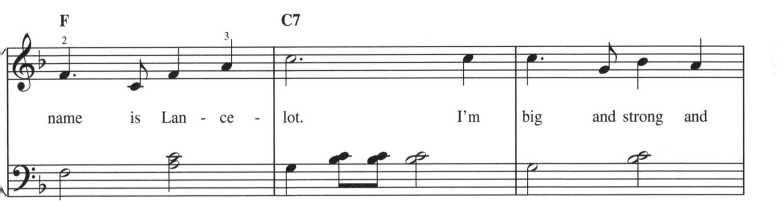

name is Lan - ce - lot. I'm big and strong and

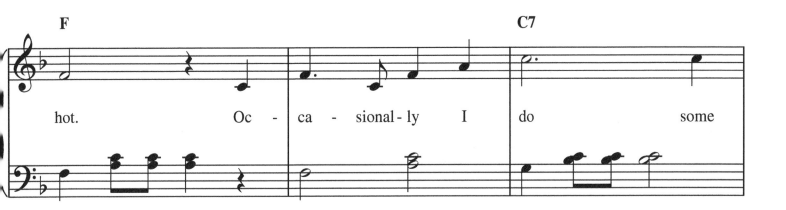

hot. Oc - ca - sional - ly I do some

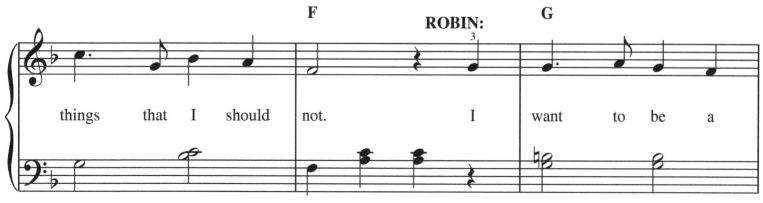

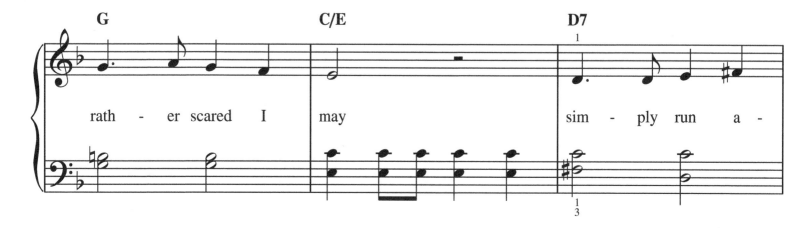

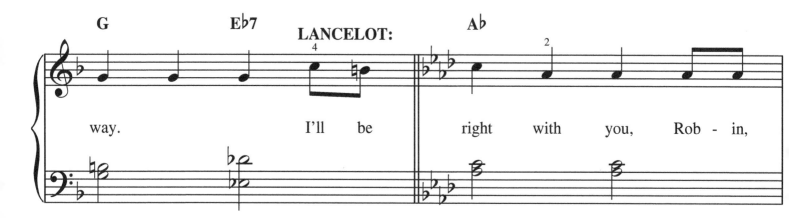

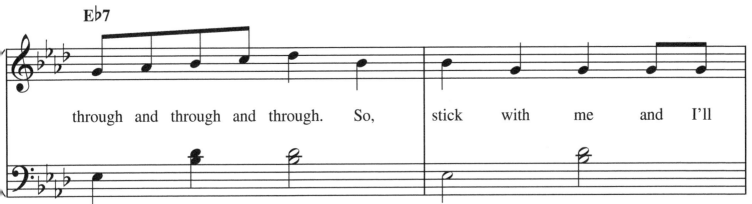

through and through and through. So, stick with me and I'll

show you what to do. **BOTH:** We'll re- main good chums. **LANCELOT:** You can

teach me how to dance. **BOTH:** We're go- ing to en- list. **ROBIN:** I'm Rob- in

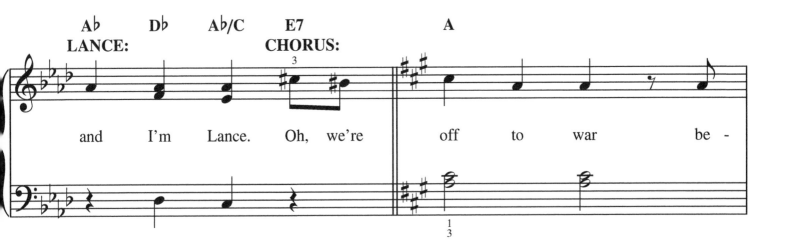

LANCE: and I'm Lance. **CHORUS:** Oh, we're off to war be-

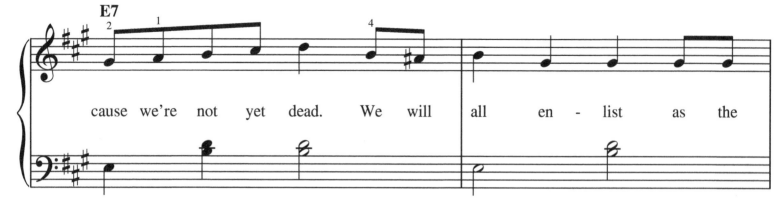

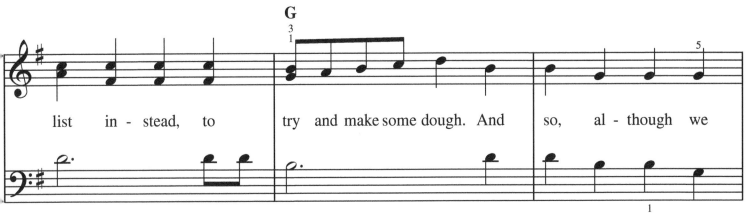

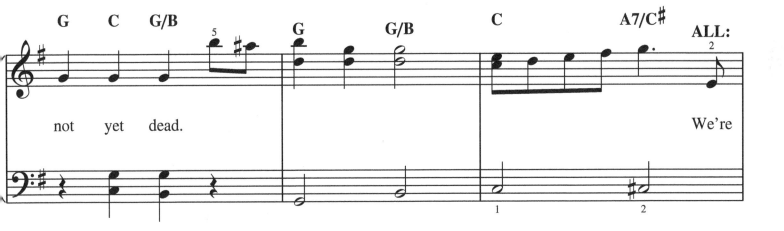

shot   by   Mi - chael   Moore,   'cause   we're   not

yet

Lancelot whacks Dad on the head again.

dead.

Not   yet   dead.

COME WITH ME

Lyrics by ERIC IDLE
Music by JOHN DU PREZ and ERIC IDLE

Gently

LADY OF THE LAKE:

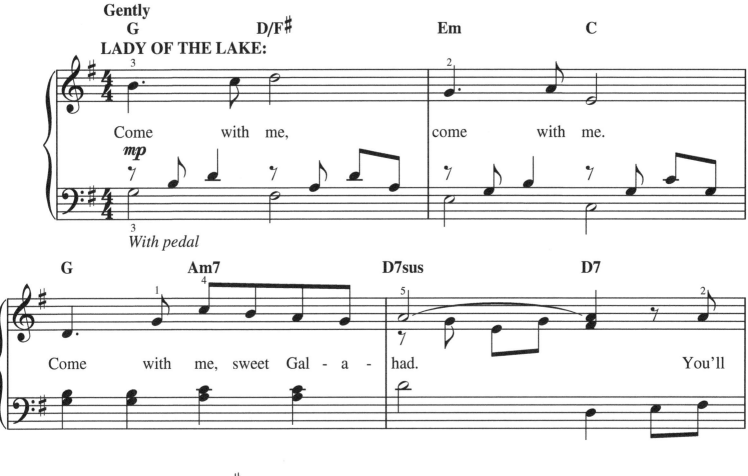

Come with me, come with me.

Come with me, sweet Gal - a - had. You'll

be a man, join Ar - thur's clan.

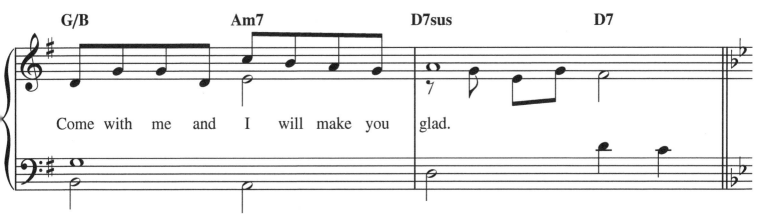

Come with me and I will make you glad.

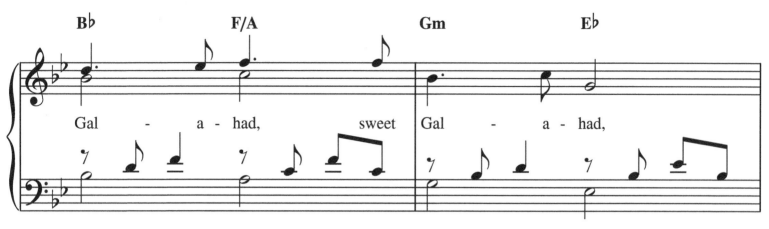

Gal - a - had, sweet Gal - a - had,

be a Knight, it's time to take your vow. If

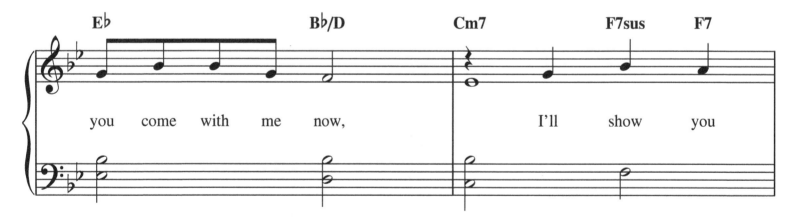

you come with me now, I'll show you

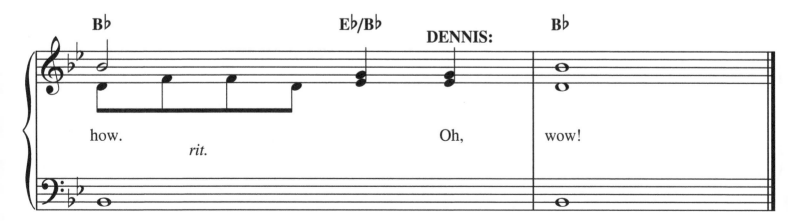

how. *rit.* **DENNIS:** Oh, wow!

THE SONG THAT GOES LIKE THIS

Lyrics by ERIC IDLE
Music by JOHN DU PREZ and ERIC IDLE

Moderately, but with great intensity

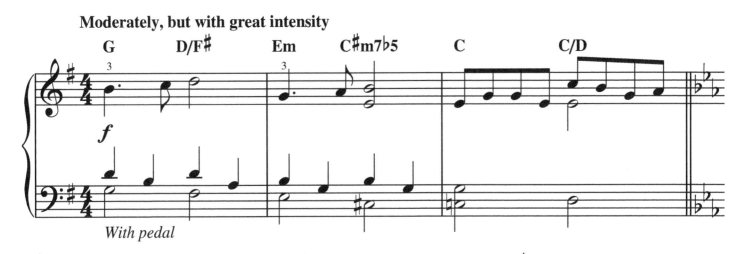

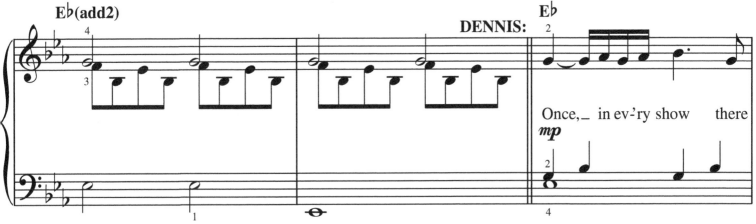

DENNIS: Once,— in ev'ry show there

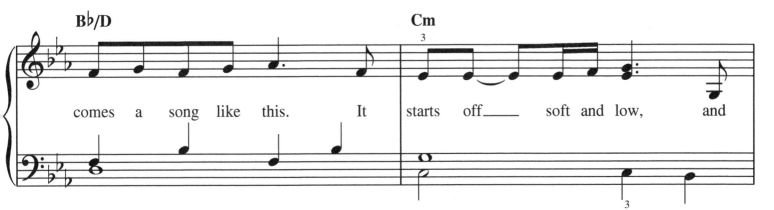

comes a song like this. It starts off— soft and low, and

ends up— with a kiss. Oh, where is the song that goes like

B♭sus ... **B♭** ... **LADY:**

this? *Where is it? Where? Where? A*

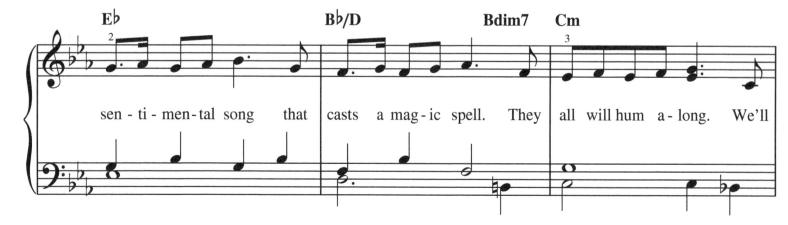

E♭ ... **B♭/D** ... **Bdim7** ... **Cm**

sen - ti - men-tal song that casts a mag - ic spell. They all will hum a - long. We'll

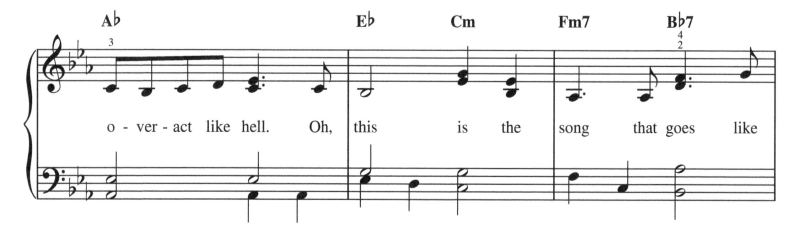

A♭ ... **E♭** ... **Cm** ... **Fm7** ... **B♭7**

o - ver - act like hell. Oh, this is the song that goes like

E♭ ... **A♭/E♭**

DENNIS: ... **LADY:** ... **DENNIS:** ... **LADY:**

this. *Yes, it is!* *Yes, it is! Yes, it is! Yes, it is!*

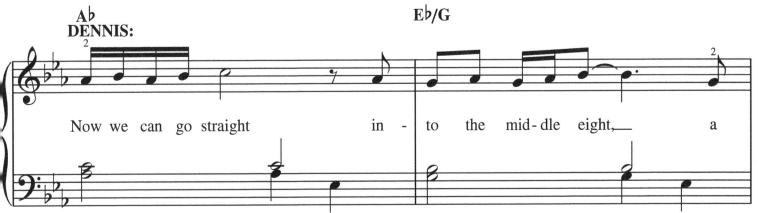

DENNIS: Now we can go straight in - to the mid - dle eight, — a

LADY: bridge that is too far for me. I'll sing it in your face,

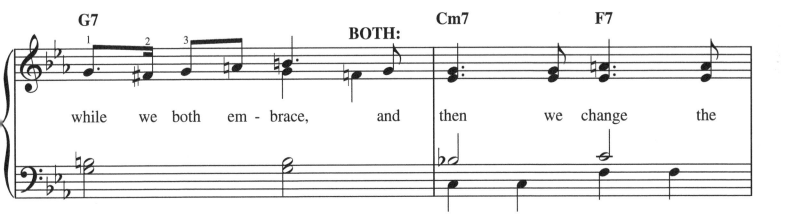

BOTH: while we both em - brace, and then we change the

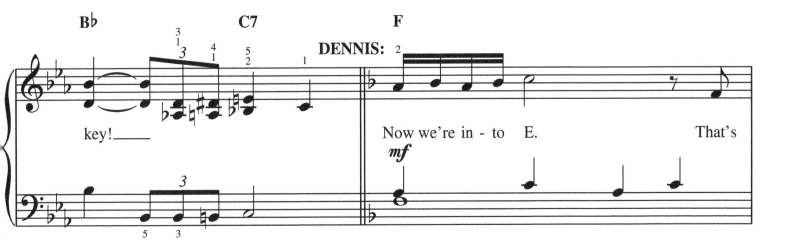

DENNIS: key! Now we're in - to E. That's

C/E — aw - fully high for me. But **LADY:** Dm ev - 'ry - one can see we

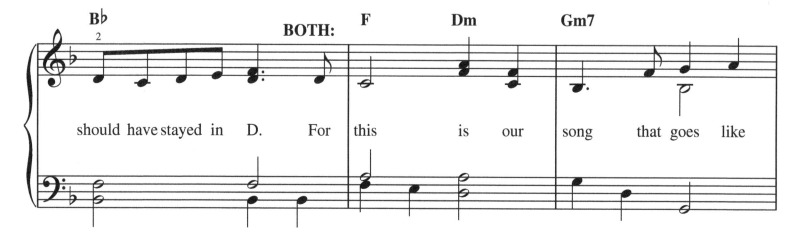

B♭ should have stayed in D. **BOTH:** F For this Dm is our Gm7 song that goes like

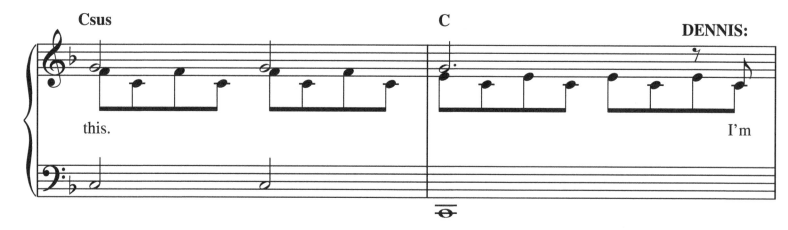

Csus this. C **DENNIS:** I'm

F feel - ing ver - y proud. **LADY:** You're C/E sing - ing far too loud. **DENNIS:** That's the

way that this song goes. **LADY:** You're stand-ing on my toes. **BOTH:** Sing - ing our

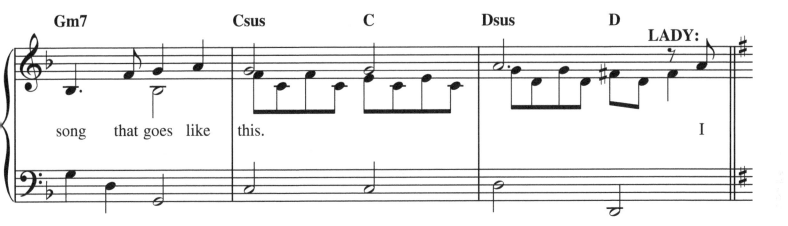

song that goes like this. **LADY:** I

can't be-lieve there's more. **DENNIS:** It's far too long, I'm sure. **LADY:** That's the

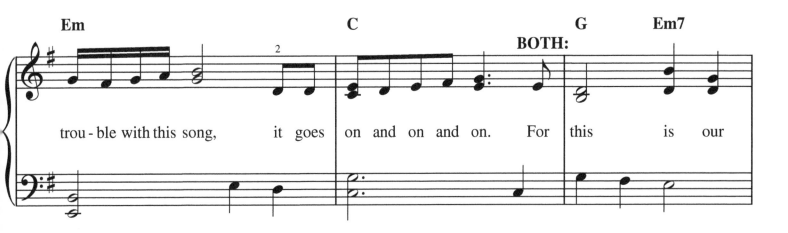

trou-ble with this song, it goes on and on and on. **BOTH:** For this is our

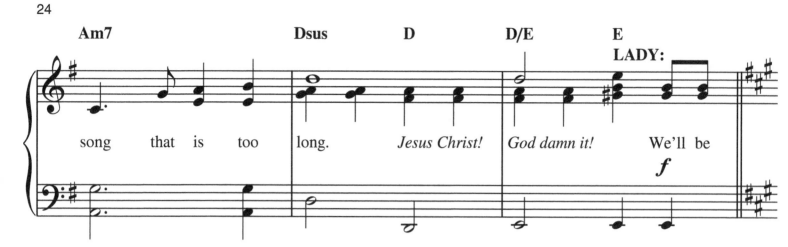

song that is too long. *Jesus Christ!* *God damn it!* We'll be

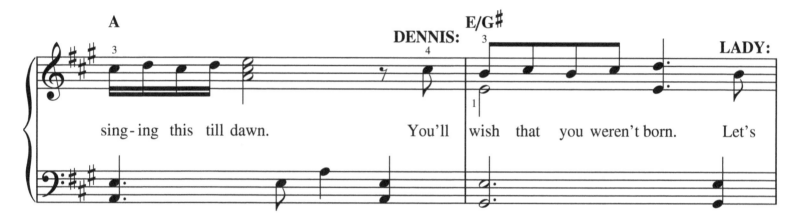

sing-ing this till dawn. You'll wish that you weren't born. Let's

stop this damn re-frain, be - fore we go in-sane. The

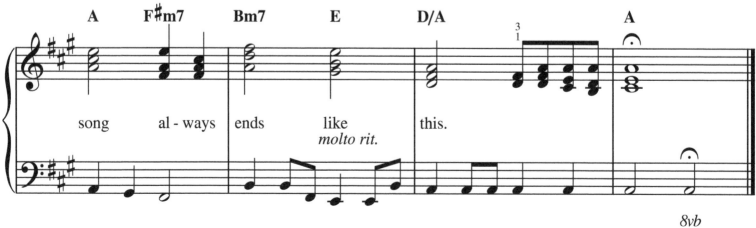

song al - ways ends like this.

molto rit.

8vb

ALL FOR ONE

Lyrics by ERIC IDLE
Music by JOHN DU PREZ and ERIC IDLE

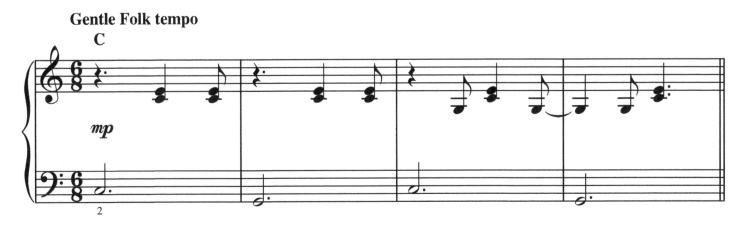

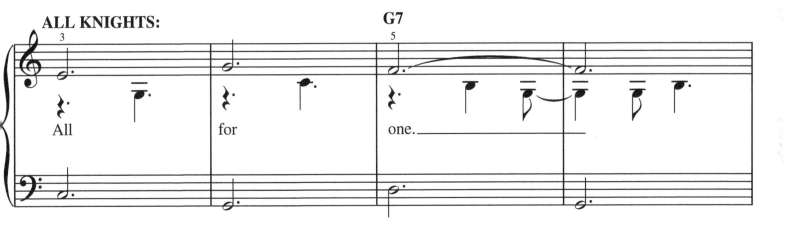

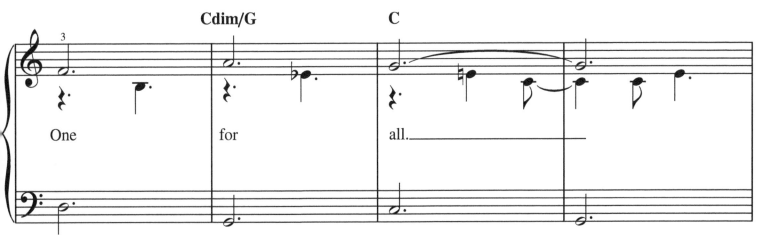

26

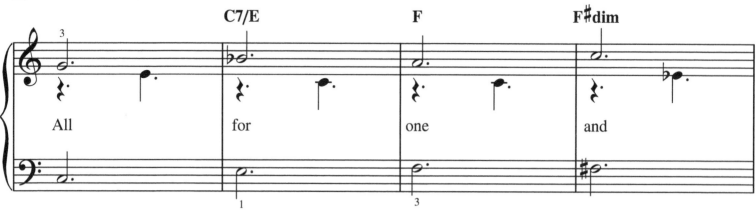

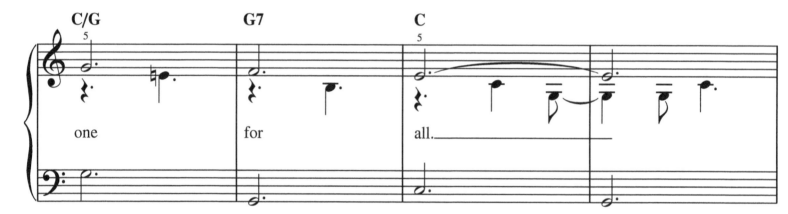

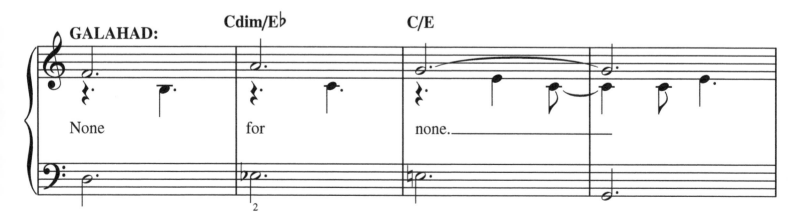

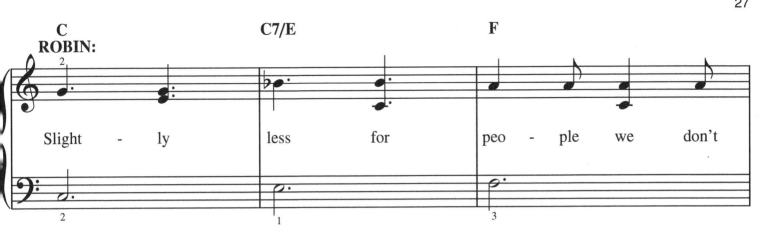

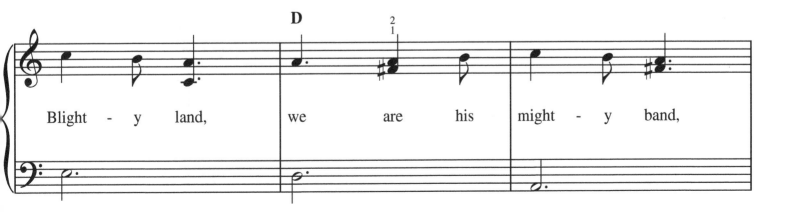

oooo. ____

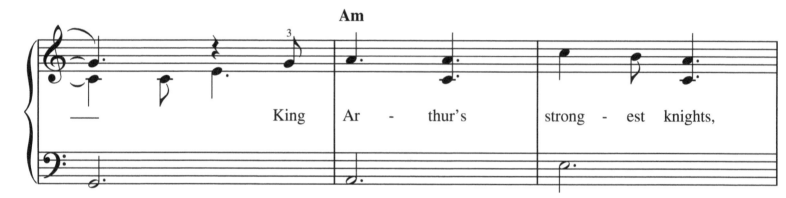

King Ar - thur's strong - est knights,

we are pre - pared to fight who -

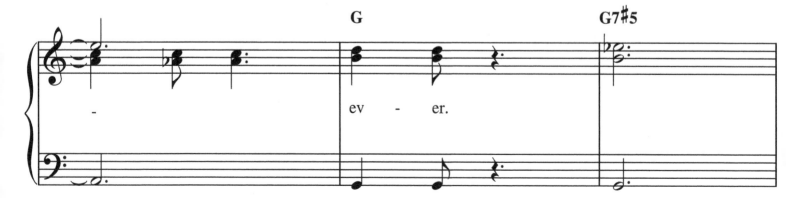

- ev - er.

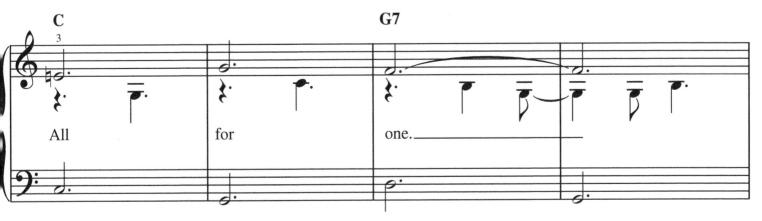

All   for   one._____

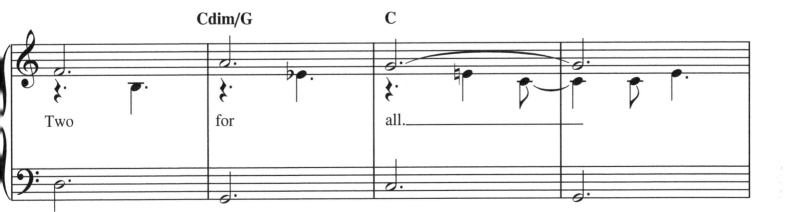

Two   for   all._____

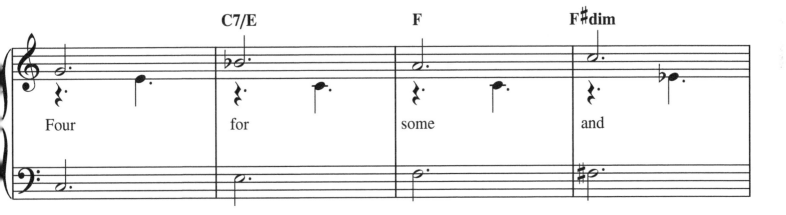

Four   for   some   and

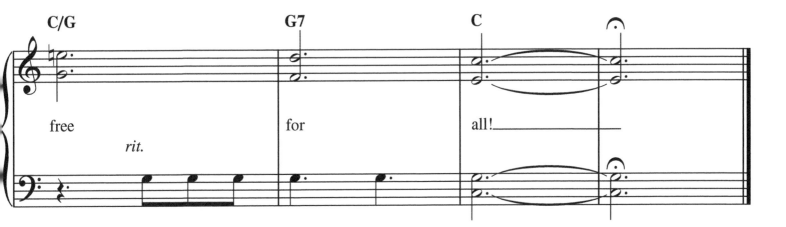

free   *rit.*   for   all!_____

KNIGHTS OF THE ROUND TABLE

Words and Music by NEIL INNES,
JOHN CLEESE and GRAHAM CHAPMAN

Brisk Show-Biz 2

We're

Knights of the Round Ta - ble, we dance when-e'er we're a - ble. { We
{ We

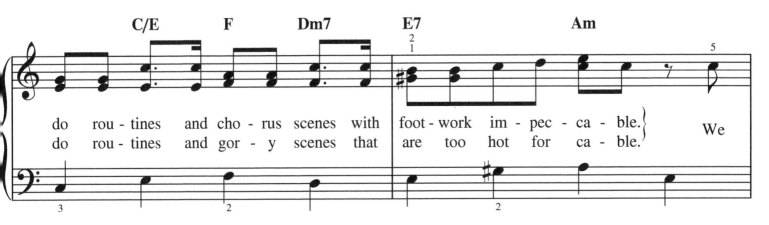

do rou - tines and cho - rus scenes with foot - work im - pec - ca - ble.
do rou - tines and gor - y scenes that are too hot for ca - ble. }

We

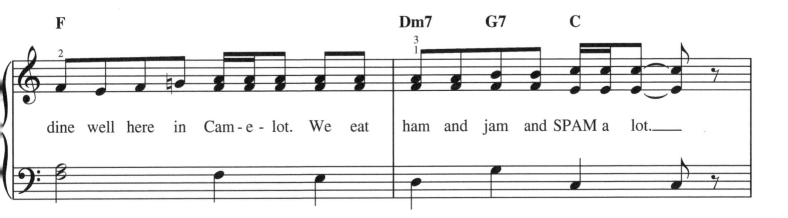

dine well here in Cam - e - lot. We eat ham and jam and SPAM a lot.____

ALL KNIGHTS:
(minus ARTHUR)

We're

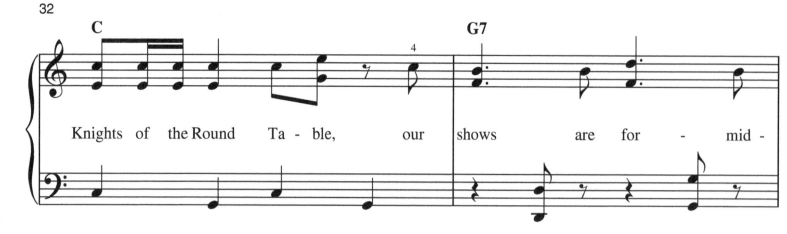

Knights of the Round Ta - ble, our shows are for - mid -

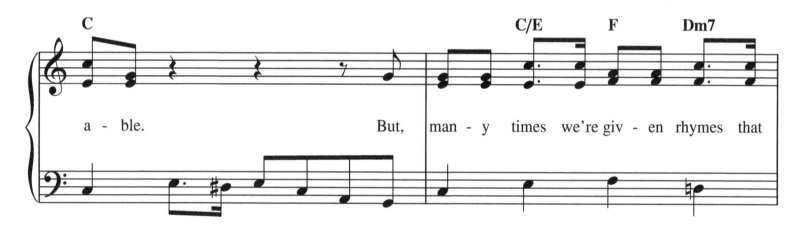

a - ble. But, man - y times we're giv - en rhymes that

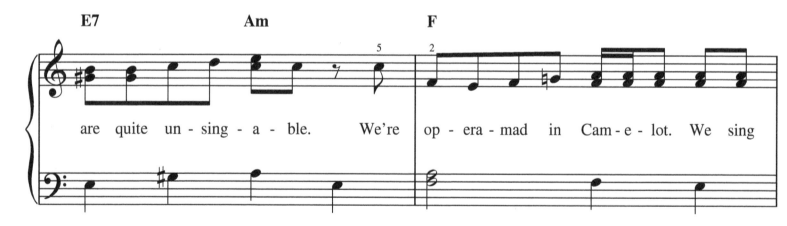

are quite un - sing - a - ble. We're op - era - mad in Cam - e - lot. We sing

from the di - a - phragm a lot.____

ALL KNIGHTS:

We're Knights of the Round Ta - ble, al -

though we live a fa - ble. We're not just bums with roy - al mums. We've

brains that are quite a - ble. We've a bus - y life in Cam - e - lot.

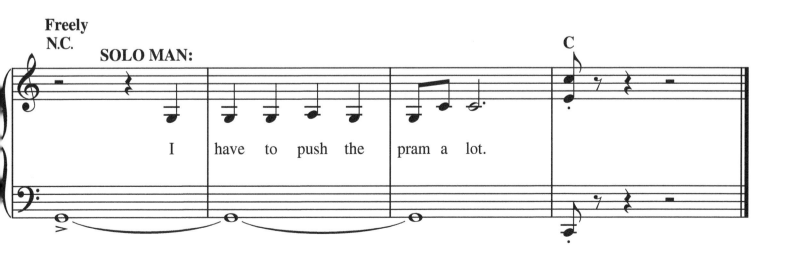

Freely
N.C.
SOLO MAN:

I have to push the pram a lot.

FIND YOUR GRAIL

Lyrics by ERIC IDLE
Music by JOHN DU PREZ and ERIC IDLE

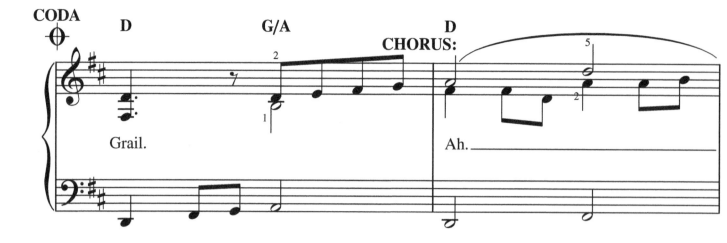

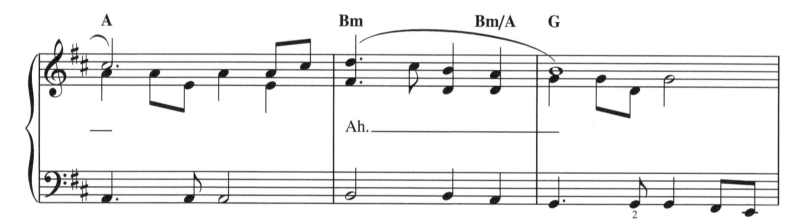

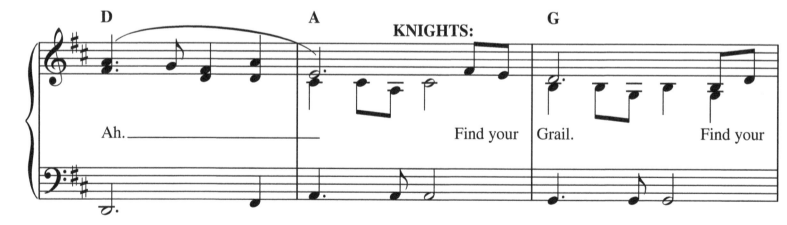

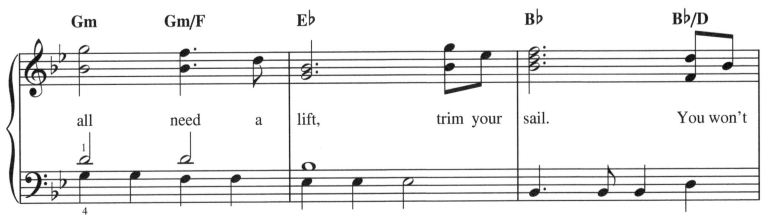

all need a lift, trim your sail. You won't

fail. Find your Grail. Find your Grail.

Life is real-ly up to you.— You must choose what to pur-sue.—

Set your mind on what to find, and there's

noth - ing you can't do, you can't

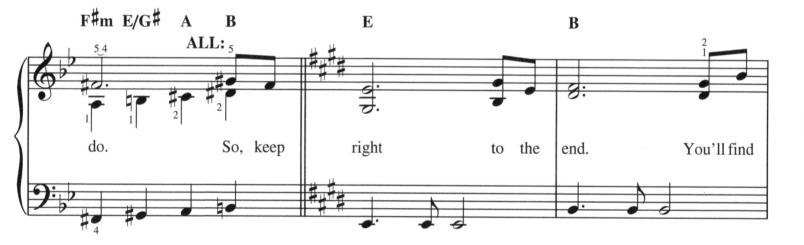

do. So, keep right to the end. You'll find

your goal, my friend. Find your Grail. You won't fail. Find your

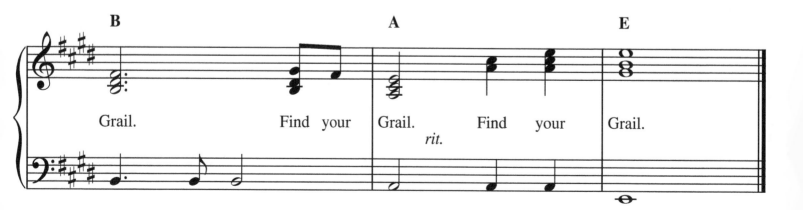

Grail. Find your Grail. Find your Grail.

rit.

RUN AWAY!

Lyrics by ERIC IDLE
Music by JOHN DU PREZ and ERIC IDLE

Can-Can tempo

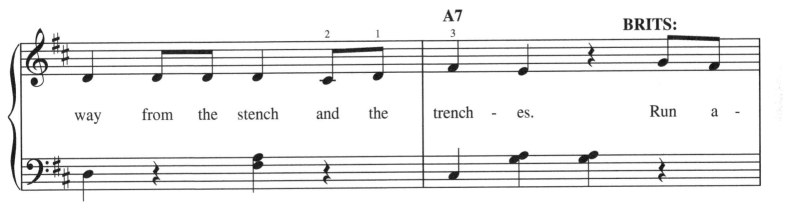

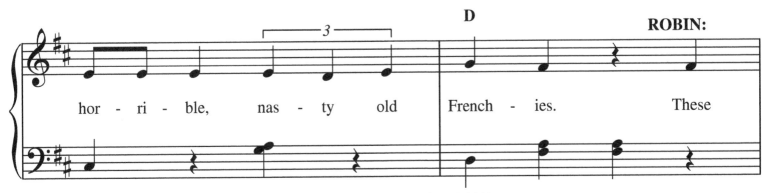

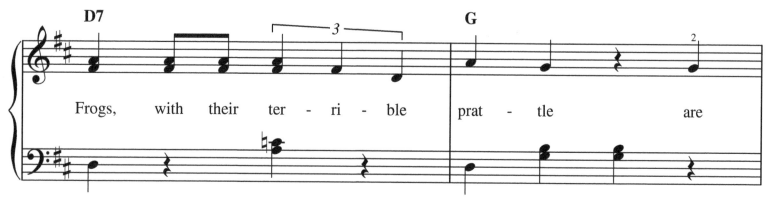

Frogs, with their ter - ri - ble prat - tle are

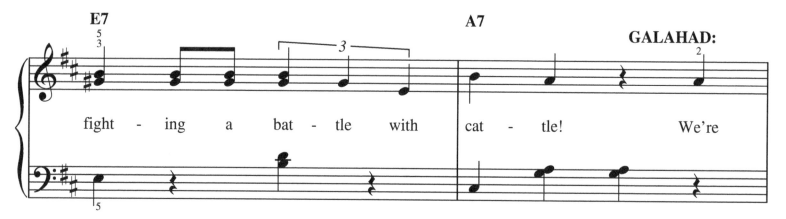

GALAHAD:

fight - ing a bat - tle with cat - tle! We're

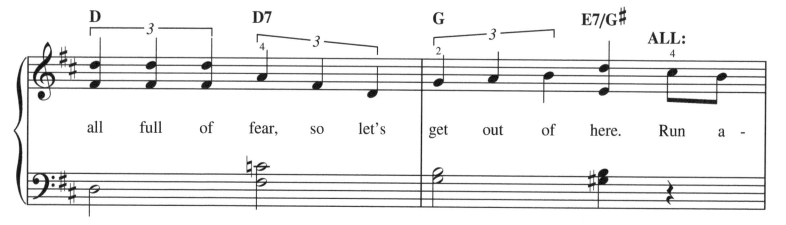

ALL:

all full of fear, so let's get out of here. Run a -

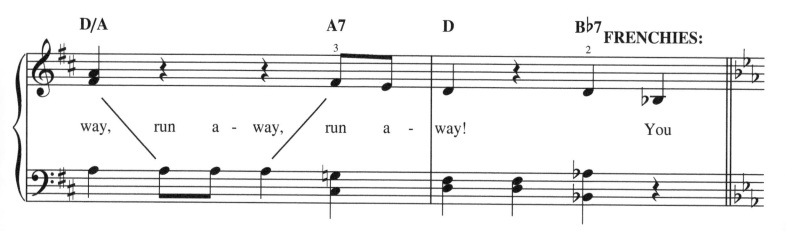

FRENCHIES:

way, run a - way, run a - way! You

English are all bug - ger folk. Your moth - ers are all

rug - ger folk. Your ar - my is a blood - y joke. You

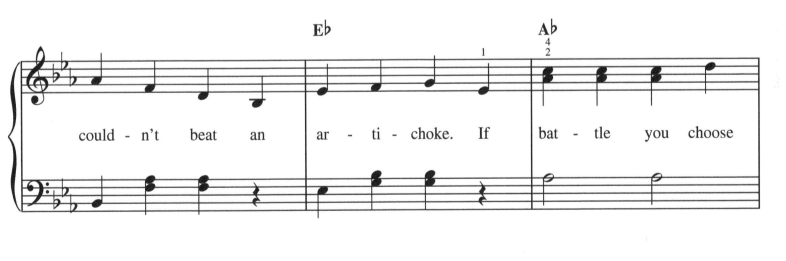

could - n't beat an ar - ti - choke. If bat - tle you choose

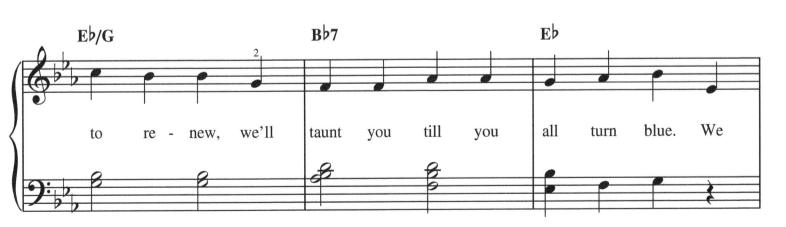

to re - new, we'll taunt you till you all turn blue. We

42

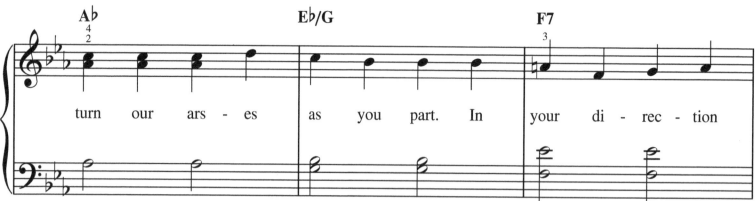

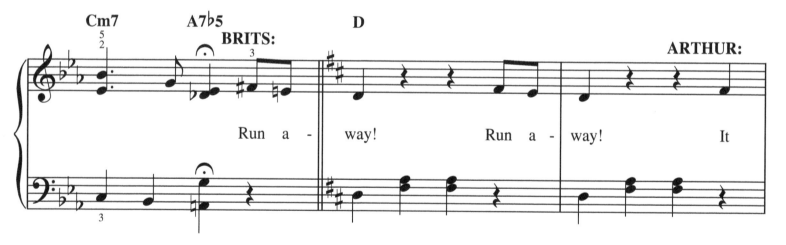

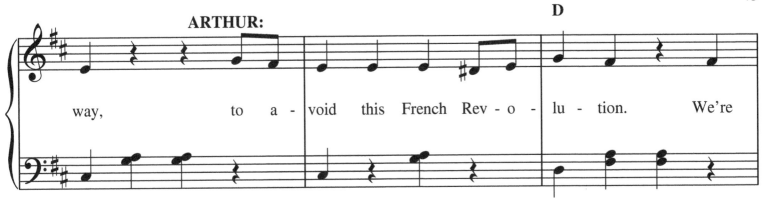

ARTHUR:
way, to a-void this French Rev-o-lu-tion. We're

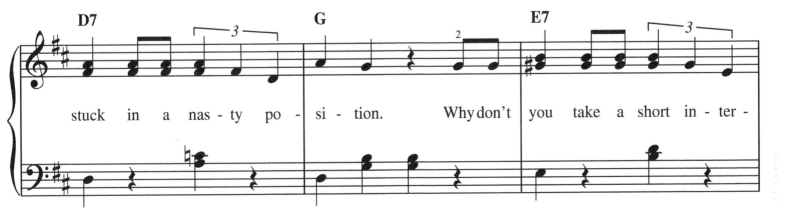

stuck in a nas-ty po-si-tion. Why don't you take a short in-ter-

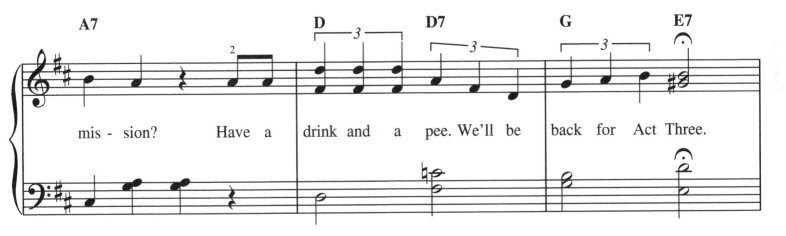

mis-sion? Have a drink and a pee. We'll be back for Act Three.

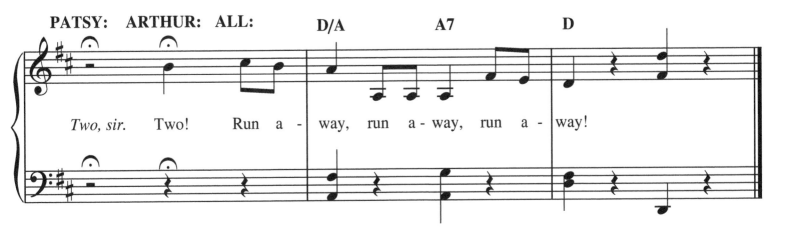

PATSY: ARTHUR: ALL:
Two, sir. Two! Run a-way, run a-way, run a-way!

ALWAYS LOOK ON THE BRIGHT SIDE OF LIFE

Words and Music by
ERIC IDLE

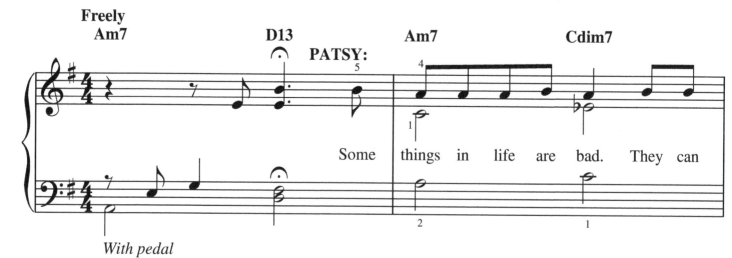

PATSY: Some things in life are bad. They can

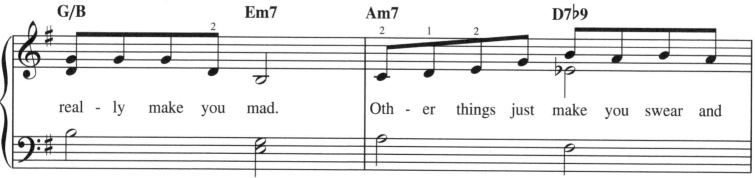

real - ly make you mad. Oth - er things just make you swear and

curse. When you're chew - in' on life's gris - tle, don't

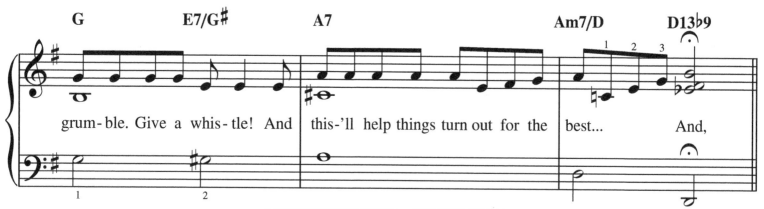

grum - ble. Give a whis - tle! And this - 'll help things turn out for the best... And,

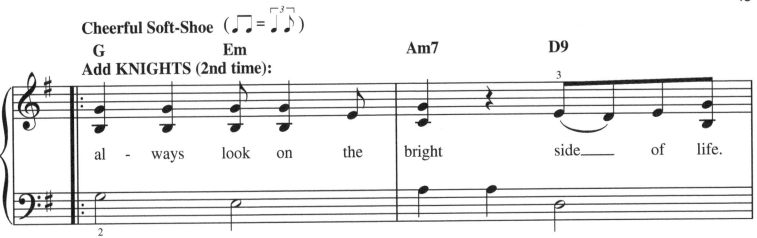

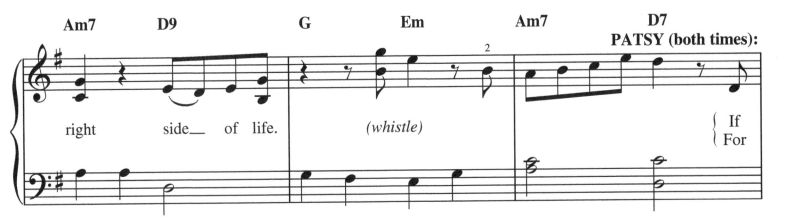

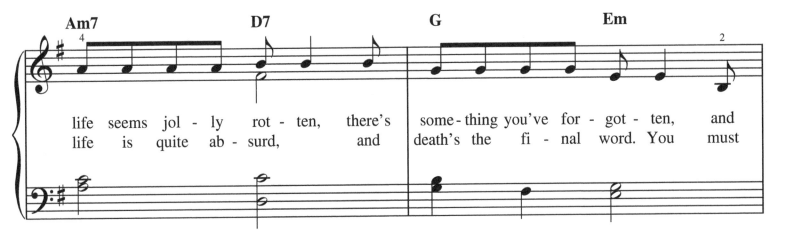

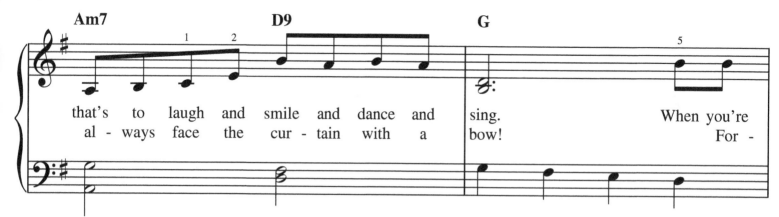

that's to laugh and smile and dance and sing. When you're
al - ways face the cur - tain with a bow! For -

feel - ing in the dumps, don't be sil - ly chumps. Just
get a - bout your sin. Give the au - di - ence a grin. En -

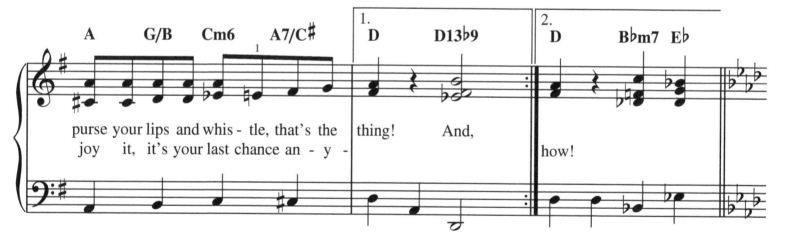

purse your lips and whis - tle, that's the thing! And,
joy it, it's your last chance an - y - how!

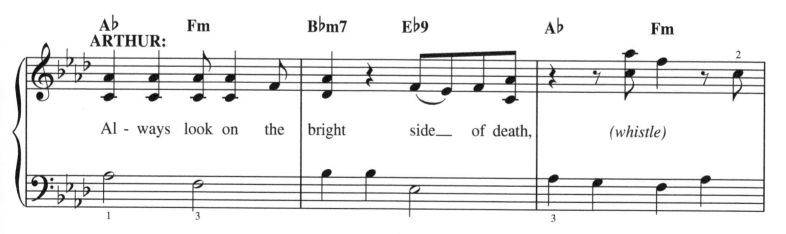

ARTHUR:
Al - ways look on the bright side__ of death, *(whistle)*

just be-fore you draw your ter-min-al breath.

(whistle)

Life's a piece of shit,

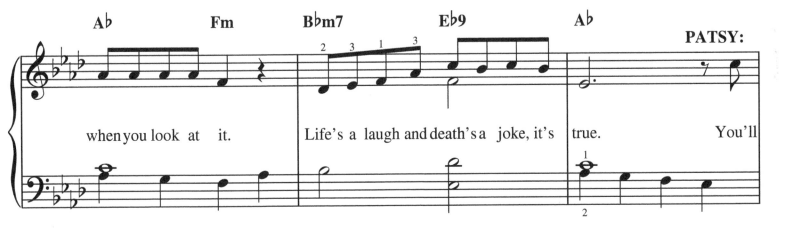

when you look at it. Life's a laugh and death's a joke, it's true. You'll

PATSY:

see it's all a show. Keep 'em laugh-ing as you go! Just re-

ARTHUR:

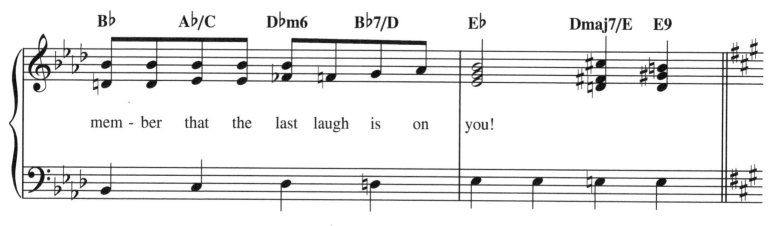

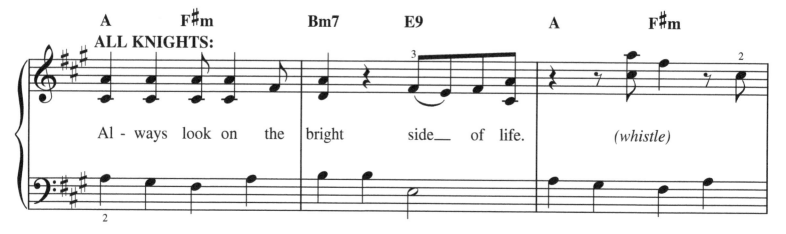

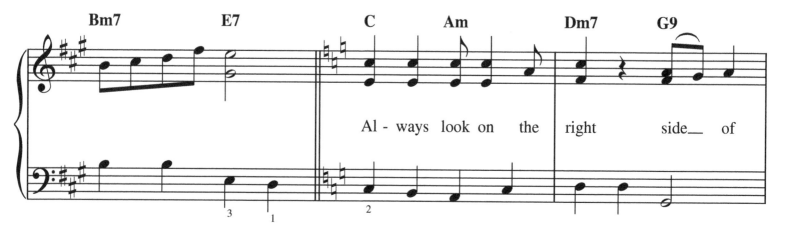

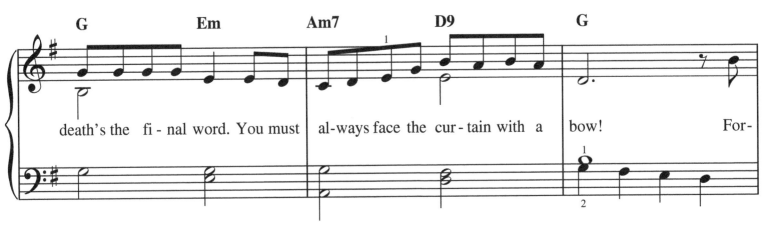

death's the fi-nal word. You must al-ways face the cur-tain with a bow! For-

get a-bout your sin. Give the au-di-ence a grin. En-

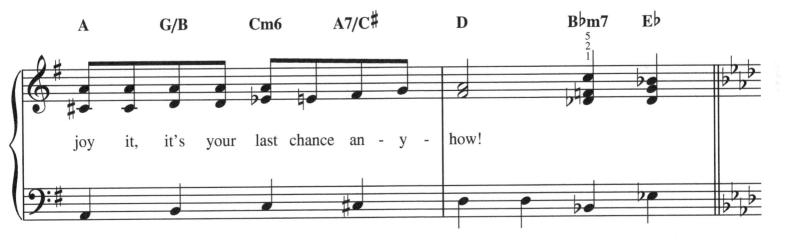

joy it, it's your last chance an-y-how!

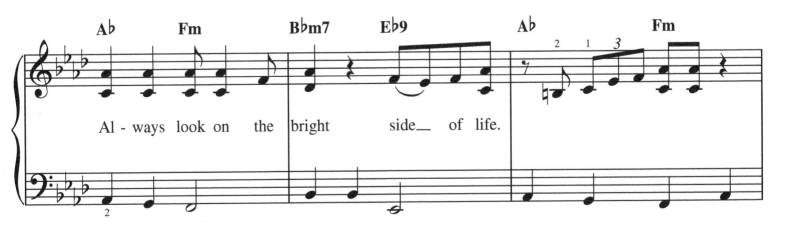

Al-ways look on the bright side— of life.

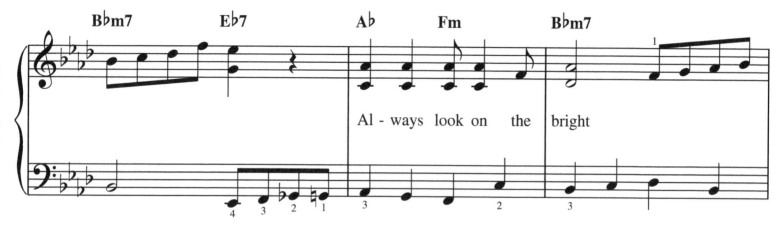

Al - ways look on the bright

side — of life,— side — of life,—

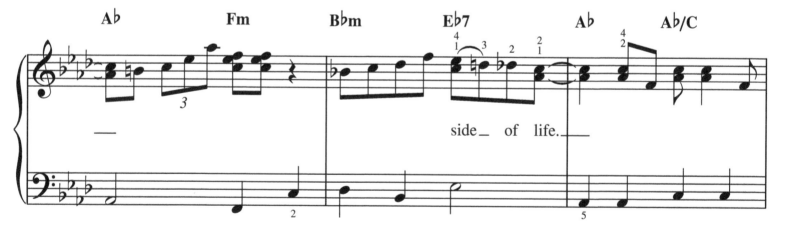

— side — of life.—

BRAVE SIR ROBIN

Words by ERIC IDLE
Music by NEIL INNES

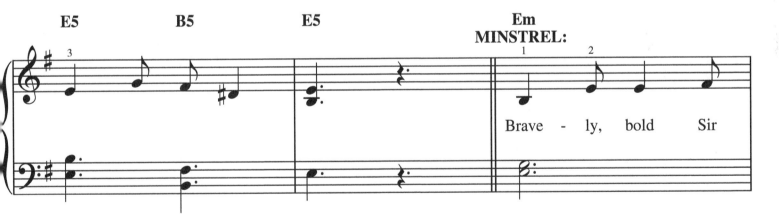

Brave - ly, bold Sir

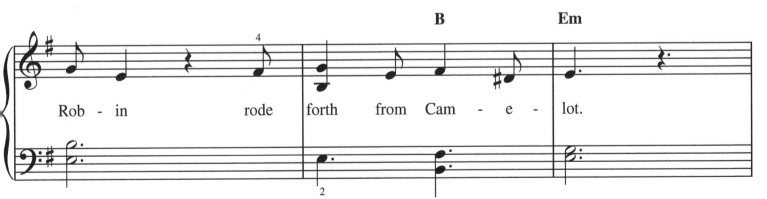

Rob - in rode forth from Cam - e - lot.

He was not a - fraid to die, O brave Sir

Rob - in._____ He was not at all a - fraid to be

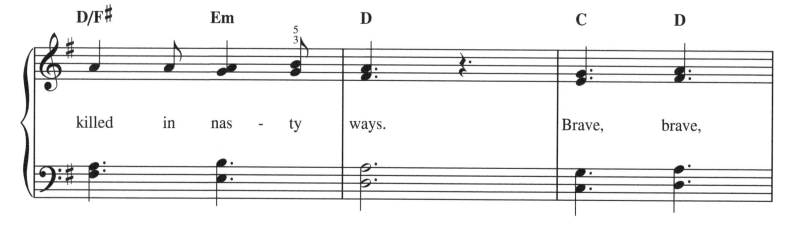

killed in nas - ty ways. Brave, brave,

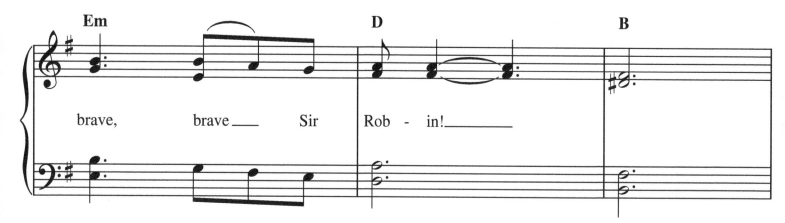

brave, brave___ Sir Rob - in!_____

He was not in the least bit scared to be mashed in-to a

pulp, or to have his eyes gouged out,

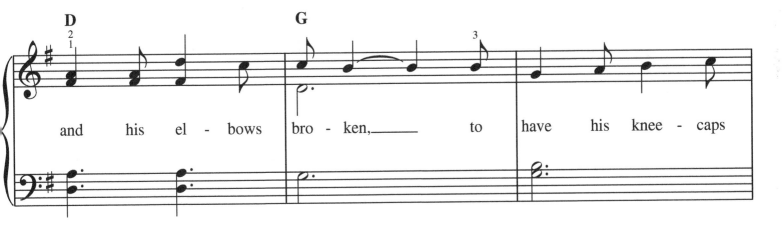

and his el - bows bro - ken,_____ to have his knee - caps

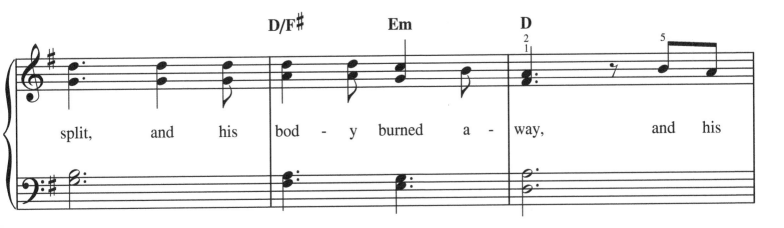

split, and his bod - y burned a - way, and his

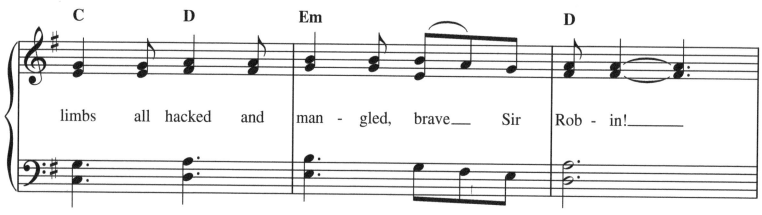

limbs all hacked and man - gled, brave___ Sir Rob - in!_____

His head smashed in and his heart cut out, and his

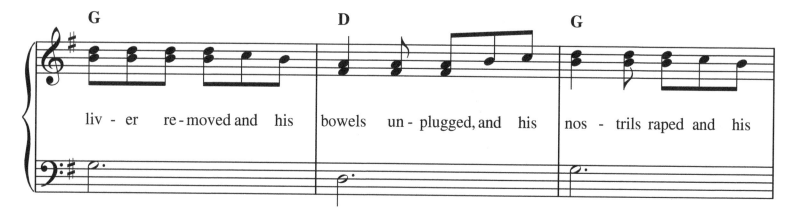

liv - er re - moved and his bowels un - plugged, and his nos - trils raped and his

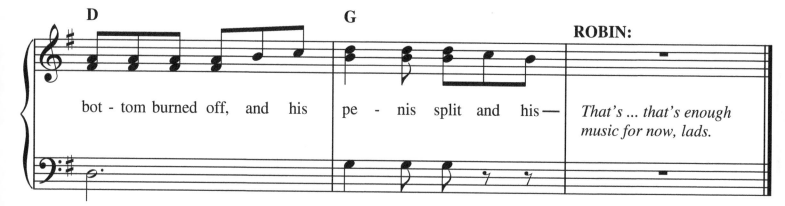

bot - tom burned off, and his pe - nis split and his— *That's ... that's enough music for now, lads.*

ROBIN:

WHATEVER HAPPENED TO MY PART?

Lyrics by ERIC IDLE
Music by JOHN DU PREZ and ERIC IDLE

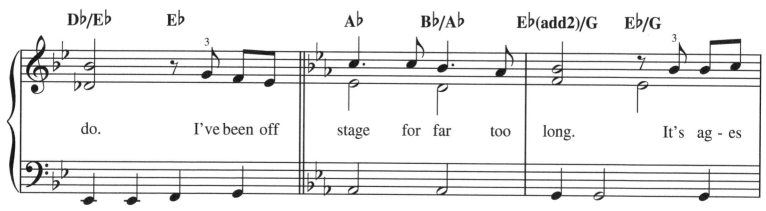

Db/Eb   Eb   Ab   Bb/Ab   Eb(add2)/G   Eb/G

do.   I've been off   stage for far too   long.   It's ag - es

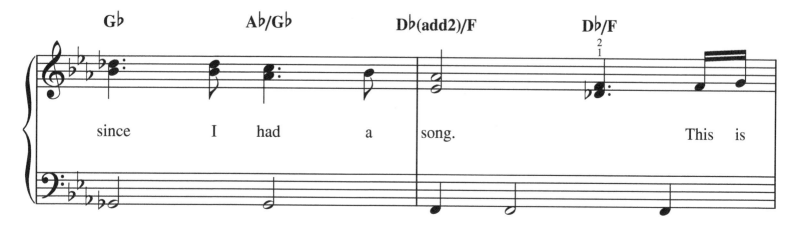

Gb   Ab/Gb   Db(add2)/F   Db/F

since   I had   a   song.   This   is

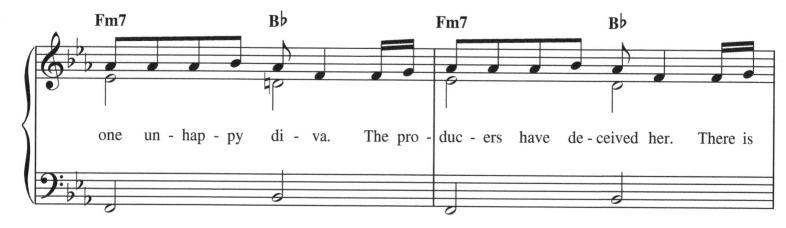

Fm7   Bb   Fm7   Bb

one un - hap - py di - va.   The pro - duc - ers have de - ceived her.   There is

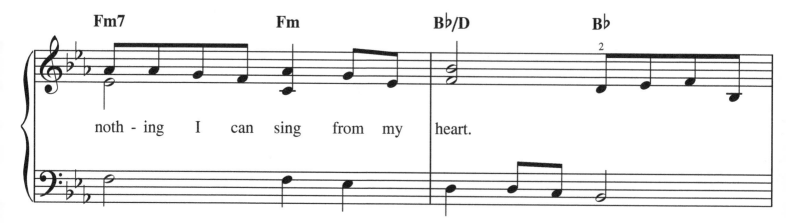

Fm7   Fm   Bb/D   Bb

noth - ing   I can sing   from my   heart.

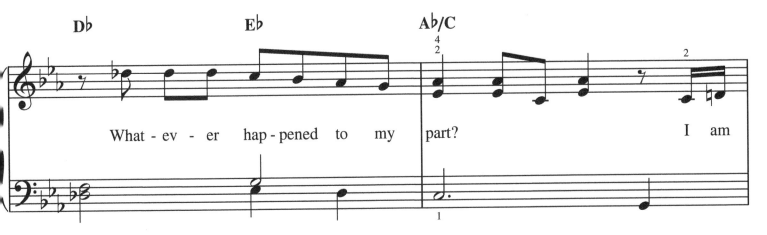

Whatever happened to my part? I am

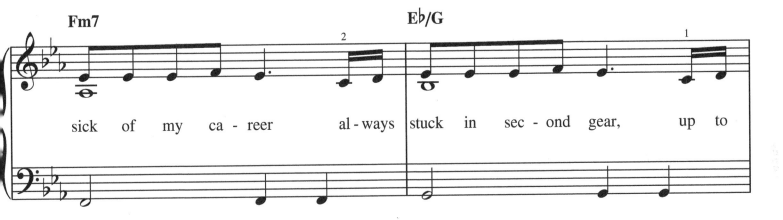

sick of my career always stuck in second gear, up to

here with frustration and with fears. I've no

Grammy, no rewards. I've no Tony Awards. I'm

Fm7

con - stant - ly re - placed by Brit - ney

B♭sus **B♭**

Spears.

LADY & GIRLS:

Brit - ney

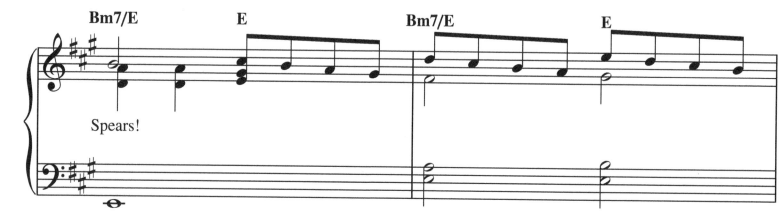

Bm7/E **E**

Spears!

Bm7/E **E**

A **G♯m7♭5** **C♯7** **F♯m** **A7**

LADY OF THE LAKE:

What - ev - er hap - pened to my show?

D **C♯m7♭5** **F♯7/A♯** **Bm** **Bm/A**

I was a hit. Now, I don't know._____ I'm with a

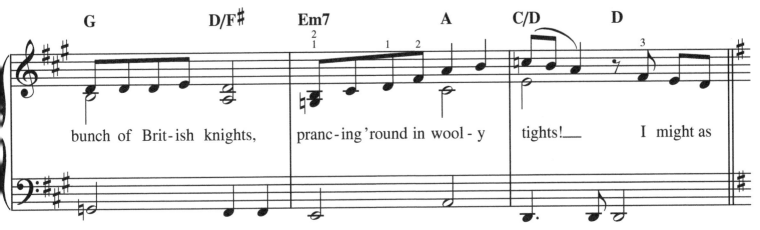

bunch of Brit-ish knights, pranc-ing 'round in wool - y tights!___ I might as

well go to the pub. They've been out

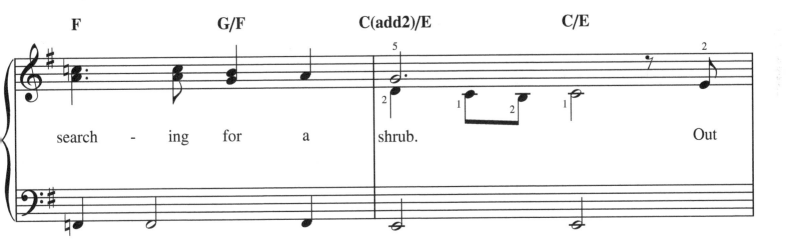

search - ing for a shrub. Out

shop - ping for a bush! Well, they can kiss my tush! It

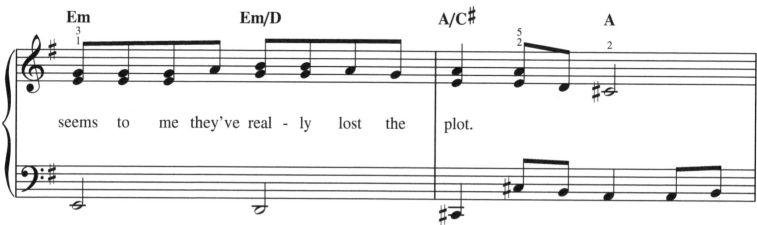

seems to me they've real - ly lost the plot.

What - ev - er hap - pened to my— I'll call my a - gent, dam - mit—

what - ev - er happened to my... *not yours... not yours...* but my_____

rit.

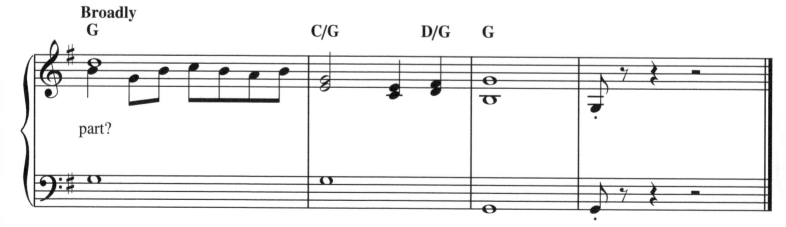

part?

HIS NAME IS LANCELOT

Lyrics by ERIC IDLE
Music by JOHN DU PREZ and ERIC IDLE

Bright Disco

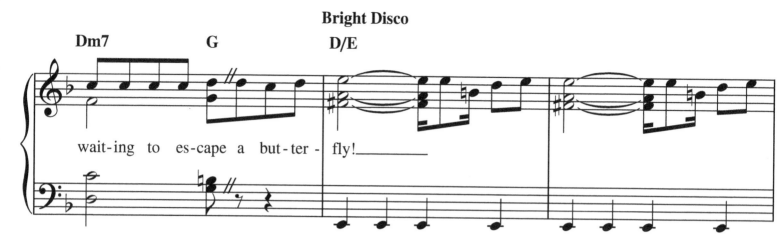

wait-ing to es-cape a but-ter - fly!_____

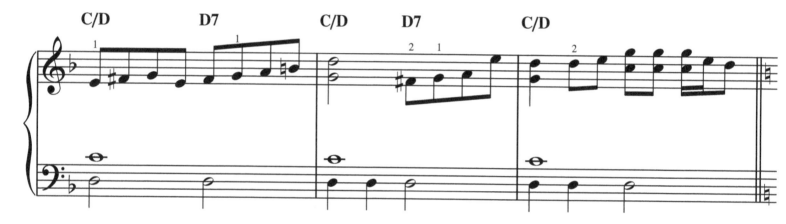

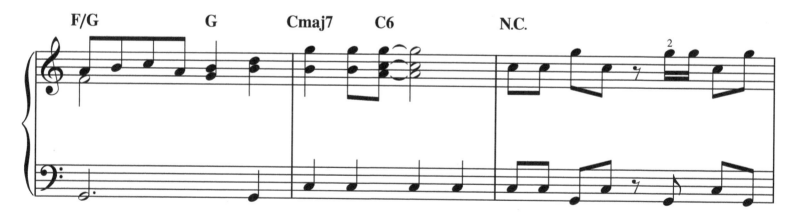

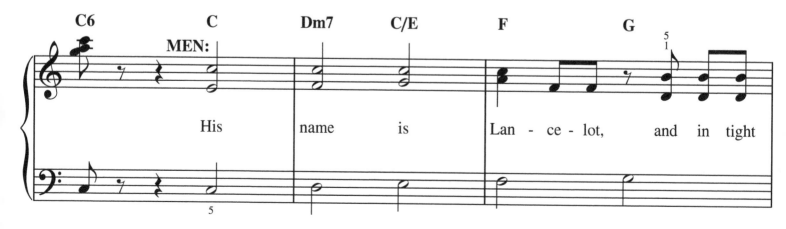

MEN: His name is Lan - ce - lot, and in tight

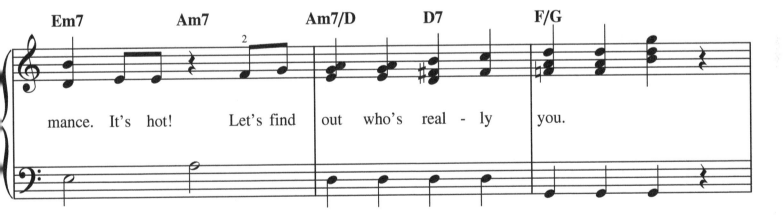

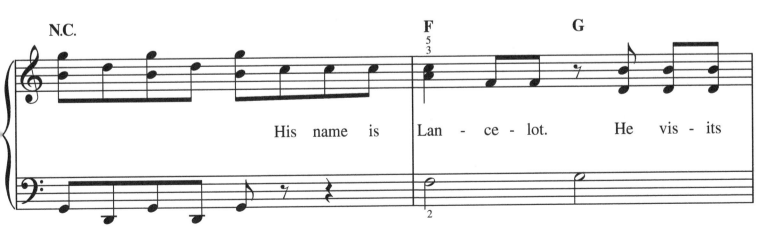

France a lot. He likes to dance a lot and dream. No one would

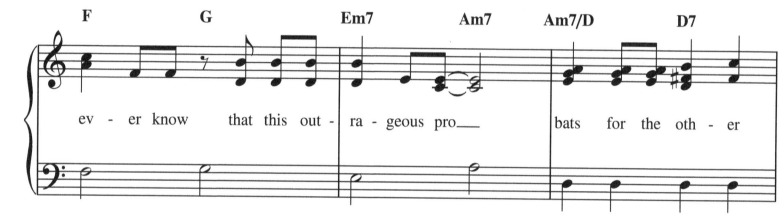

ev - er know that this out - ra - geous pro___ bats for the oth - er

team. You're a knight who real - ly likes his night life,

and by day you real - ly like to play. You can all find him

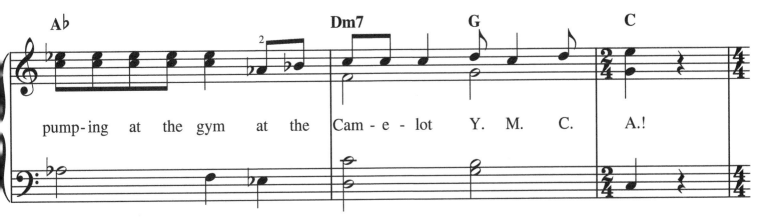

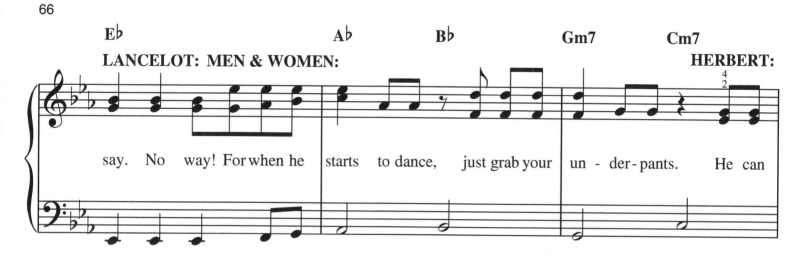

I'M ALL ALONE

Lyrics by ERIC IDLE
Music by JOHN DU PREZ and ERIC IDLE

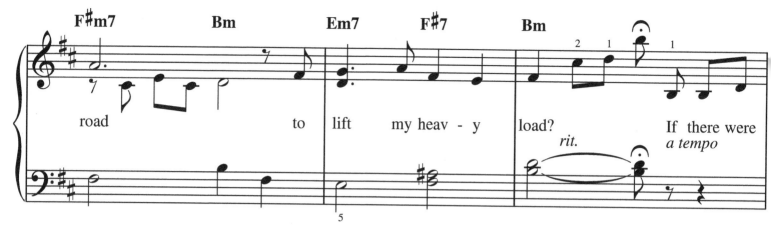

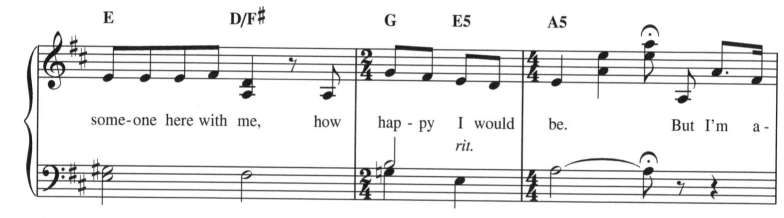

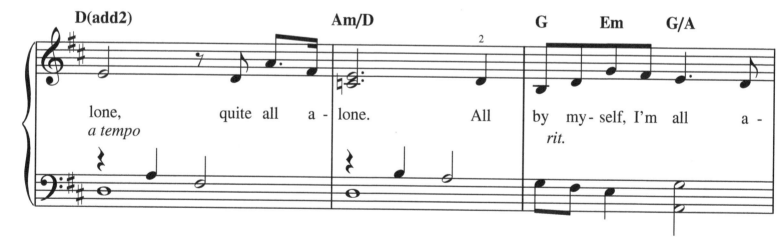

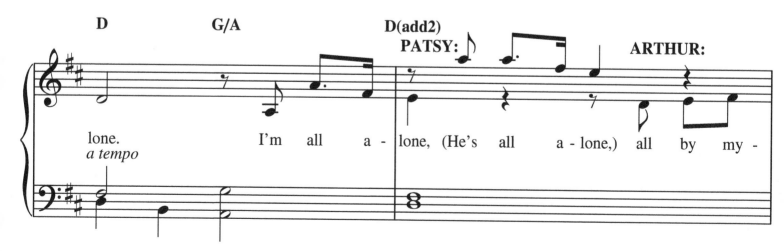

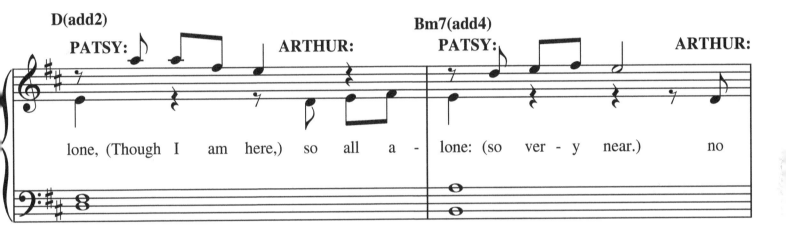

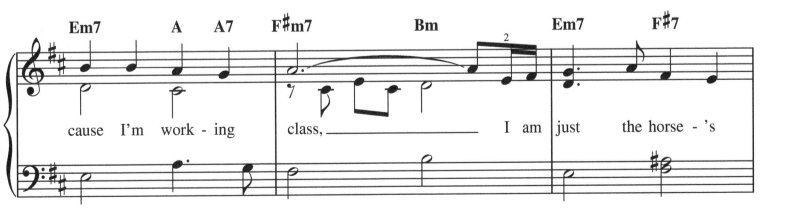

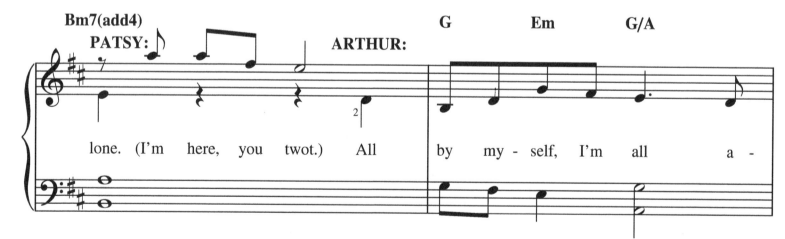

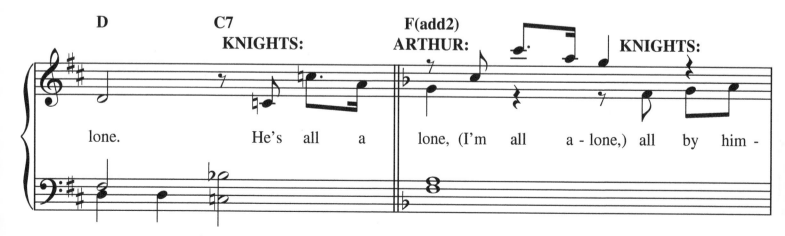

Dm7(add4)
ARTHUR: **KNIGHTS:**   **Gm7**

self. (all by my - self.) There is   no   one   here   be -

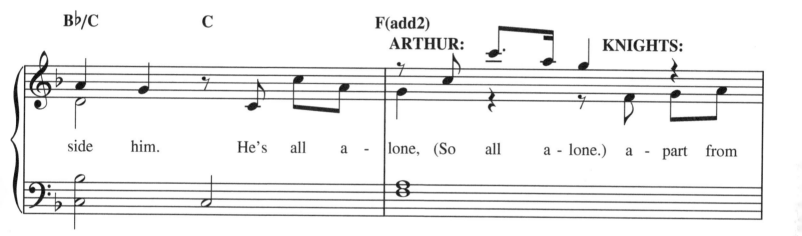

Bb/C   **C**   **F(add2)**
                                          ARTHUR: **KNIGHTS:**

side him.   He's all a - lone, (So   all   a - lone.) a - part from

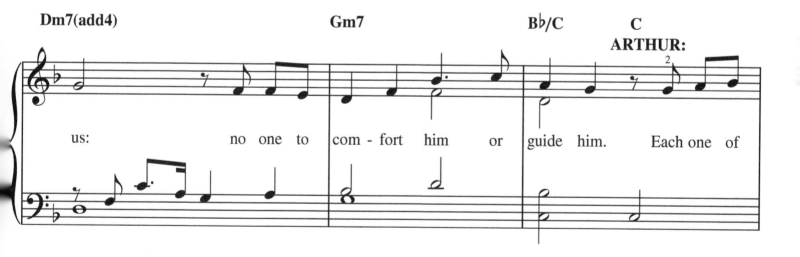

Dm7(add4)   **Gm7**   **Bb/C**   **C**
                                                                     ARTHUR:

us: no one to   com - fort him   or   guide him.   Each one of

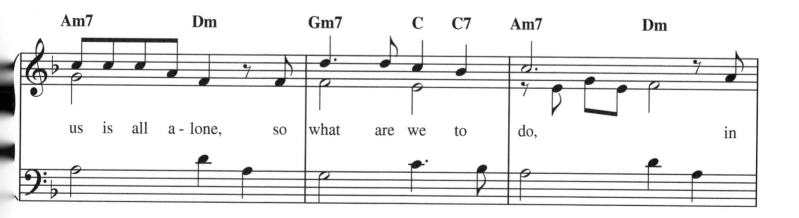

Am7   **Dm**   **Gm7**   **C C7**   **Am7**   **Dm**

us is all a - lone,   so   what   are we to   do,   in

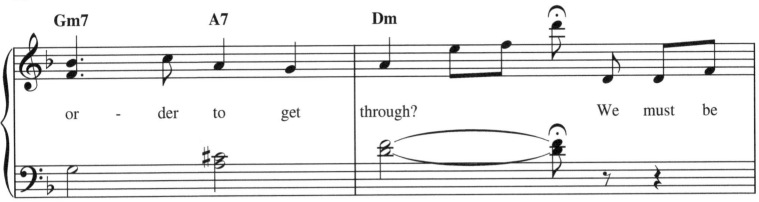

or - der to get through? We must be

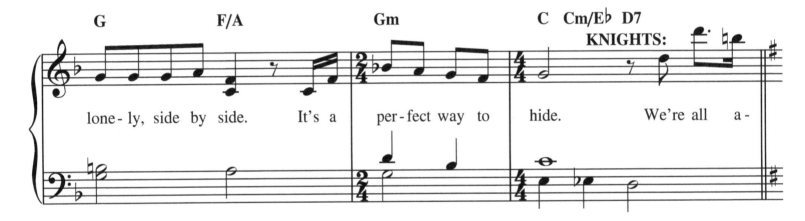

G F/A Gm C Cm/Eb D7
KNIGHTS:

lone - ly, side by side. It's a per-fect way to hide. We're all a-

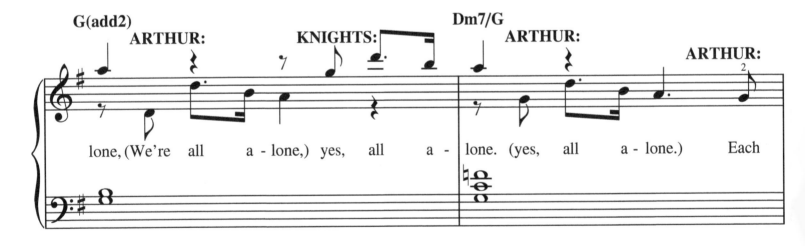

G(add2) Dm7/G
ARTHUR: KNIGHTS: ARTHUR: ARTHUR:

lone, (We're all a - lone,) yes, all a - lone. (yes, all a - lone.) Each

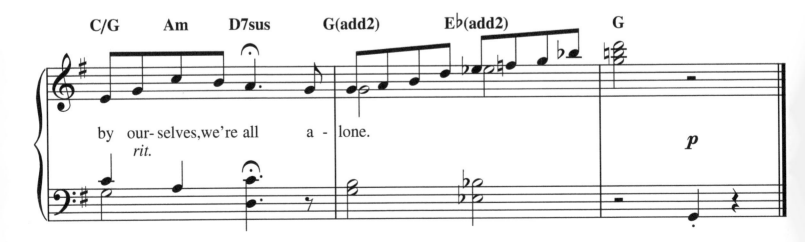

C/G Am D7sus G(add2) Eb(add2) G

by our-selves, we're all a - lone.
rit.

p